WHAT I HATE

BY THE SAME AUTHOR

A Friend for Marco*
Too Busy Marco*
Theories of Everything
The Party, After You Left
Childproof
Mondo Boxo
Proof of Life on Earth
The Four Elements
Parallel Universes
Unscientific Americans
Poems and Songs
Last Resorts

* children's books

WHAT I HATE

FROM A TO Z

ROZ CHAST

BLOOMSBURY

NEW YORK   BERLIN   LONDON   SYDNEY

Published by Bloomsbury USA, New York

All papers used by Bloomsbury USA are natural, recyclable products made
from wood grown in well-managed forests. The manufacturing processes
conform to environmental regulations of the country of origin.

Library of Congress Cataloging-in-Publication Data

Chast, Roz.
What I hate: from A to Z / Roz Chast. — 1ST U.S. ed.
p. cm.
ISBN 978-1-60819-689-0
1. American wit and humor, Pictorial. I. Title.
NC 1429. C525A4 2011
741. 5'6973 — dc 22
2011010410

First U.S. Edition 2011

1 3 5 7 9 10 8 6 4 2

Printed in the U.S.A. by Quad/Graphics, Taunton

Introduction

■   ■   ■

I'M PRETTY SURE OF TWO THINGS ABOUT MYSELF. The first is that I am an anxious person. I come from a long line of anxious people, so this doesn't surprise me. One of the first abstract terms I remember learning was *anxiety*, which for years I thought was pronounced "ANG-zhuh-tee," because, I suppose, it wasn't a word I heard very often from my fellow four-year-olds. The second thing is that I know the alphabet by heart, which is handy, because sometimes when it's taking too long to fall asleep, and I'm sick of my thoughts running around pointlessly like overtired, sweaty, cranky children, I play the Alphabet Game in the hope that as I'm playing, all those thoughts will settle down so I can get some sleep.

Here's how you play: Pick a category with which you are at least slightly familiar and try to list one thing per letter in alphabetical order. Some of my favorite categories are rock bands, fruits and vegetables, prescription drugs, countries, diseases, flowers, birds, and movie titles. You can use the same categories night after night. It doesn't matter. I have a friend who lists couples she knows who have divorced. It's an anti-insomnia game, not a Smartest Person contest, so you don't want to make it too challenging.

Anyway, one night I was lying in bed and waiting to fall asleep. I was letting my thoughts run around, hoping they'd tire themselves out. As often happens when I'm lying in the dark, my thoughts drifted to various "concerns," the word my father used for his anxieties. I thought about rooftop swimming pools filled with heavy, heavy water; the age and possible decrepitude of the bridges and tunnels that subway trains ran over or through; the continued existence of my appendix; wires in the walls; our boiler; the person my parents knew who had been killed by a flowerpot falling out of a window; various upcoming medical exams; cyclopia (thanks, Google Images); and various other things. At some point, I wondered whether I actually had an aversion for every letter of the alphabet.

It turns out I did.

Roz Chast

TO MY PARENTS,
ELIZABETH AND GEORGE

For many years, I thought that people who claimed to have been abducted by aliens were either desperate attention-seekers or just nuts. Why else would they say that they were spirited out of their beds and through walls and roofs and into a flying saucer? I changed my mind after attending an abductee conference. Maybe they were lunatics, but that doesn't mean they weren't onto something.

■　　■　　■

ALIEN ABDUCTION

I've been fascinated by U.F.O.s since I was a kid, when I read dozens of books about them.

I always wanted to see one, but the only place they appeared was in my dreams.

Back then, I didn't think about who (or what) would be piloting the aircraft, or why.

LOOK! A U.F.O.!

That's a PLANE, you ninny.

That came later.

Many terrible things begin with *B*: bears, blindness, boilers, bats, bridges, and brain tumors. But no one brings any of those things to a party to up the fun quotient. When I look at a balloon, all I see is an imminent explosion. Where's the fun in that?

■   ■   ■

A huge crowd of moronic-looking people hell-bent on "amusement"; brutish carnies running rigged games in which people try to win hideous stuffed animals; dangerous rides where you get flung around to the point of nauseousness, manned by drunken half-wits; electrical cables underfoot; carcinogenic food; and much, much more.

■   ■   ■

I believe that most doctors take their Hippocratic oath seriously. That they *want* to help. But sometimes, the desire to find something wrong ("in its early stages") and then see if it can be cured ("with the latest technology") can lead to trouble.

■　　■　　■

The perfect storm of claustrophobia, acrophobia, and agoraphobia.

■   ■   ■

ELEVATORS

You can get stuck by yourself.

You can get stuck with a crowd.

You can get stuck with a psycho.

And then there's the obvious.

What is a plane but a large metal container, thousands and thousands of feet up, suspended by nothing?

■   ■   ■

What if you're lying on the operating table, aware—i.e., watching, hearing, and smelling everything? But you've been paralyzed by the anesthesia, so you can't call out? And what if the anti-memory drug that is part of your anesthesia cocktail then erases this experience? Except it's not really erased. It's just been buried really deeply, like a ticking time bomb.

■　　■　　■

Picture yourself standing on the edge of a great height, say a cliff or the roof of a tall building. Your head lolls, you're dizzy, your knees buckle. Are you preparing to pass out—or jump?

■   ■   ■

The main thing about illness is that you don't know which way it's going to go. When I'm sick, I always wonder: Is this a cold? Or is it an incurable malady I picked up the other day when I rode the subway and held on to the pole and then bought a bag of mini-pretzels that I ate *without first washing my hands?*

■　　■　　■

Sometimes, things turn out in an unexpected way.

■   ■   ■

There used to be a dessert called Jell-O 1-2-3. It was made pretty much like regular Jell-O. Add water to powder, stir, chill. When chilled, it was supposed to separate into three approximately equal-sized layers, like so: →

foamy topping ←
mousse-like layer ←
base of regular Jell-O ←

However, when **I** made it, this is how it turned out. I still don't know why.

→ weird spider-webby substance creeping up sides of glass

→ thin mousse layer
→ miniscule Jell-O layer

It was so HORRIFYING that I never made it again.

JELL-O 1-2-3

R. Chr

When I was little, I was terrified of kites. I think this may have had something to do with an uncle who told me that he knew of a kid who was flying a kite, and then the wind picked up the kid with the kite, and they both disappeared into the sky. Maybe that's why.

■　　■　　■

Before I got a GPS, if I missed my highway exit, or if there was a detour because of an accident or construction and I had to *go a new way*, I'd usually get so lost that I'd wind up weeping in a parking lot somewhere. Sometimes, even if I was on the right road, I would convince myself that the road looked "different" and change course and then wind up forty miles out of the way.

■   ■   ■

According to the *World Book*, "meat is the muscle, connective tissue, and fat of animals." I eat meat, at least for now, even though I know this. Would I eat a cat or a dog? I don't think so, but why not, if I eat cows and chickens? Meat is meat, right?

■   ■   ■

There's nothing you can do to prevent nightmares, unless you decide that you're never going to sleep again. Once you slip away into the Dream World, a giant wave might be about to crash on top of you, or you're in a foreign city and you've lost the name of your hotel, and on top of that, you have nine fingers on each hand.

■　　■　　■

When that planchet starts traveling across the board, either someone is being a jerk, or you're opening a door that should really, really stay closed.

■   ■   ■

 UIJA BOARDS

Yeah. I know. They're probably bogus.

But I've had a couple of creepy experiences with them.

Why tempt fate?

When I was a child, mausoleums comforted me. I imagined that inside that little stone house was a stone bench on which the deceased, who was not in a coffin but wrapped in a sheet of some kind, would be laid out. Then, if for some reason the person was still alive, he or she could get up and bang on the door, and a cemetery worker would come and let him or her out. Crisis averted.

■   ■   ■

Quicksand is a mixture of sand or silt, clay, and salt water. A bed of quicksand will look solid, but it's not. It's more of a gel, and because of the way those things are mixed, it has some peculiar properties. When you step on it, you sink. To get out requires a lot of force. If that force isn't nearby, and you have stepped in quicksand, you might as well give up.

■   ■   ■

My rabies fear started with *To Kill a Mockingbird*, the same way my appendicitis fear started with *Madeline*, and my brain tumor fear started with *Death Be Not Proud*. On an ideal planet, children's books wouldn't be censored for references to sex, but for illnesses.

．　　．　　．

So many disturbing things begin with S: snakes, spiders, sinkholes, sharks. The thing about SHC is that even if you are in an anxious mood and you don't want to leave the house, you still aren't safe. You could be sitting in your favorite, most comforting chair, reading a book or quietly folding origami, and BOOM.

■   ■   ■

SPONTANEOUS HUMAN COMBUSTION

The combustee is usually seated in a chair.

Then suddenly —

KABLAMMO

Within a four-foot-wide circle, everything is INCINERATED.

But two feet away, a pile of newspapers is not even singed.

Most tunnels were built before there were even computers. And there's all of that water on top of them. But there you are, in your car, pretending you're just driving down any road, no problem.

■   ■   ■

You could be playing in the waves, not even in over your head, and suddenly you feel a tug. It's not your brother/sister/friend/cousin messing with you. It is the ocean, pulling you to your watery grave.

■　　■　　■

If I'm in a restaurant or a theater, and the lights start dimming, my first thought is *I am going blind.*

■   ■   ■

The first time I ever saw a water bug, I was walking along Fourteenth Street in Manhattan in maybe 1978. I grew up in Brooklyn, so I had seen lots of cockroaches. This bug was like a mega-cockroach. It was walking along the sidewalk not like a bug, but more like a small dog or a squirrel. It reminded me of something an exterminator had told a friend of mine about rats: "A rat looks at you like *you* is the problem."

■　　■　　■

If I start thinking about all the stuff going on in my body—the veins and arteries moving all that blood around, the muscles and bones, all those globby organs squishily sitting atop one another, twenty-eight feet of intestines, the brain and the larynx and everything else, it makes me feel a little sick. There's a good reason that our skin is not transparent: It's to keep us from feeling completely grossed out every time we look down at our bodies.

Also, radiation is not our friend.

■　■　■

Need I say more?

But it's more complicated than that.

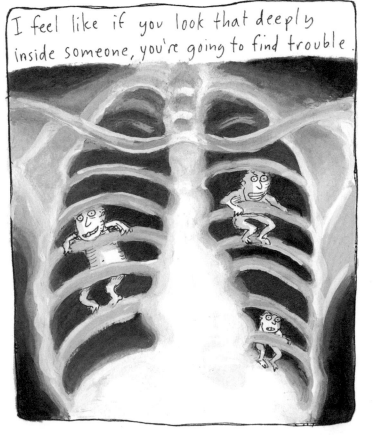

My least favorite primary color. Too bright, almost shrill.
Falsely cheerful. I admit that I like the amber hue of the
"caution" traffic light, and certain pale yellows are okay.
But in general, yellow and I are not friends.

■   ■   ■

Yellow

Yellow jacket

Yellow fever *

(*also: jaundice and hepatitis)

Cowardice

Urine

Yellowed teeth

Traffic hazards

NO PASSING

ROAD CHAOS

SLOW

DETOUR

CAUTION: FALLING ROCKS

Yellow journalism

EIGHT FATAL ILLNESSES YOU PROBABLY HAVE:

1. ~~~~   5. ~~~~
2. ~~~~   6. ~~~
3. ~~~   7. ~~~~
4. ~~~~   8. ~~~

Yellow dwarf, which is what our Sun is, which means it's dying.

R.Chst

The end. Is there light at the end of the tunnel? Or is it just nothingness? All I know for sure is, if you're talking about our alphabet, like it or not, you've come to the end of the trail.

■   ■   ■

APPENDIX

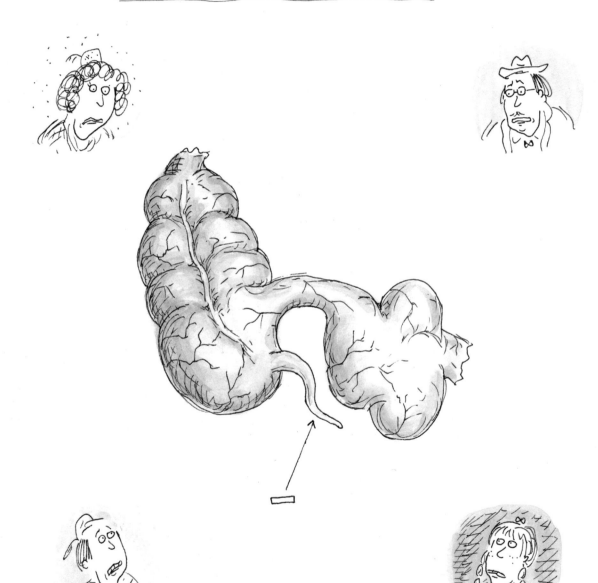

A Note on the Author

. . .

Roz Chast was born in Brooklyn, New York. Her cartoons began appearing in the *New Yorker* in 1978. Since then, she has published scores of them and written or illustrated more than a dozen books.